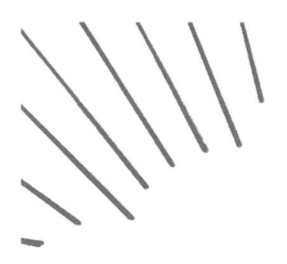

# ANTI-BULLYING
# BOOK FOR GIRLS

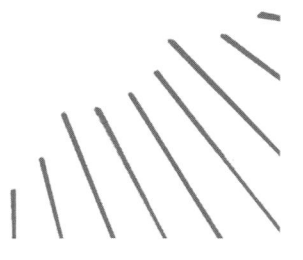

# ANTI-BULLYING BOOK

## for GIRLS

### PRACTICAL TOOLS *to* MANAGE BULLYING *and* BUILD CONFIDENCE

JESSICA WOODY

ILLUSTRATED BY MARY KATE MCDEVITT

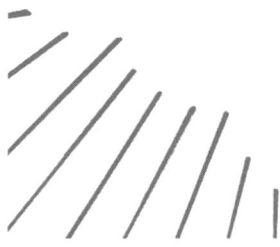

ROCKRIDGE
PRESS

For general information on our other products and services or to obtain technical support, please contact our Customer Care Department within the United States at (866) 744-2665, or outside the United States at (510) 253-0500.

Rockridge Press publishes its books in a variety of electronic and print formats. Some content that appears in print may not be available in electronic books, and vice versa.

Interior and Cover Designer: Regina Stadnik
Art Producer: Hannah Dickerson
Editor: Andrea Leptinsky
Production Editor: Emily Sheehan
Production Manager: Michael Kay

Illustrations © Mary Kate McDevitt 2021
Author photo courtesy of Summer Nicole Photography

Paperback ISBN: 978-1-63807-911-8
eBook ISBN: 978-1-63807-265-2
R0

To my parents for always telling me
I could do big things.

To my husband for his tremendous
amount of love and support.

To my sweet M and G—no matter what
struggles come your way, I hope you hold
your head high and know how loved
you truly are.

To my students—you are more powerful
than you think. Be nice, include others,
and stand united against bullying.

# CONTENTS

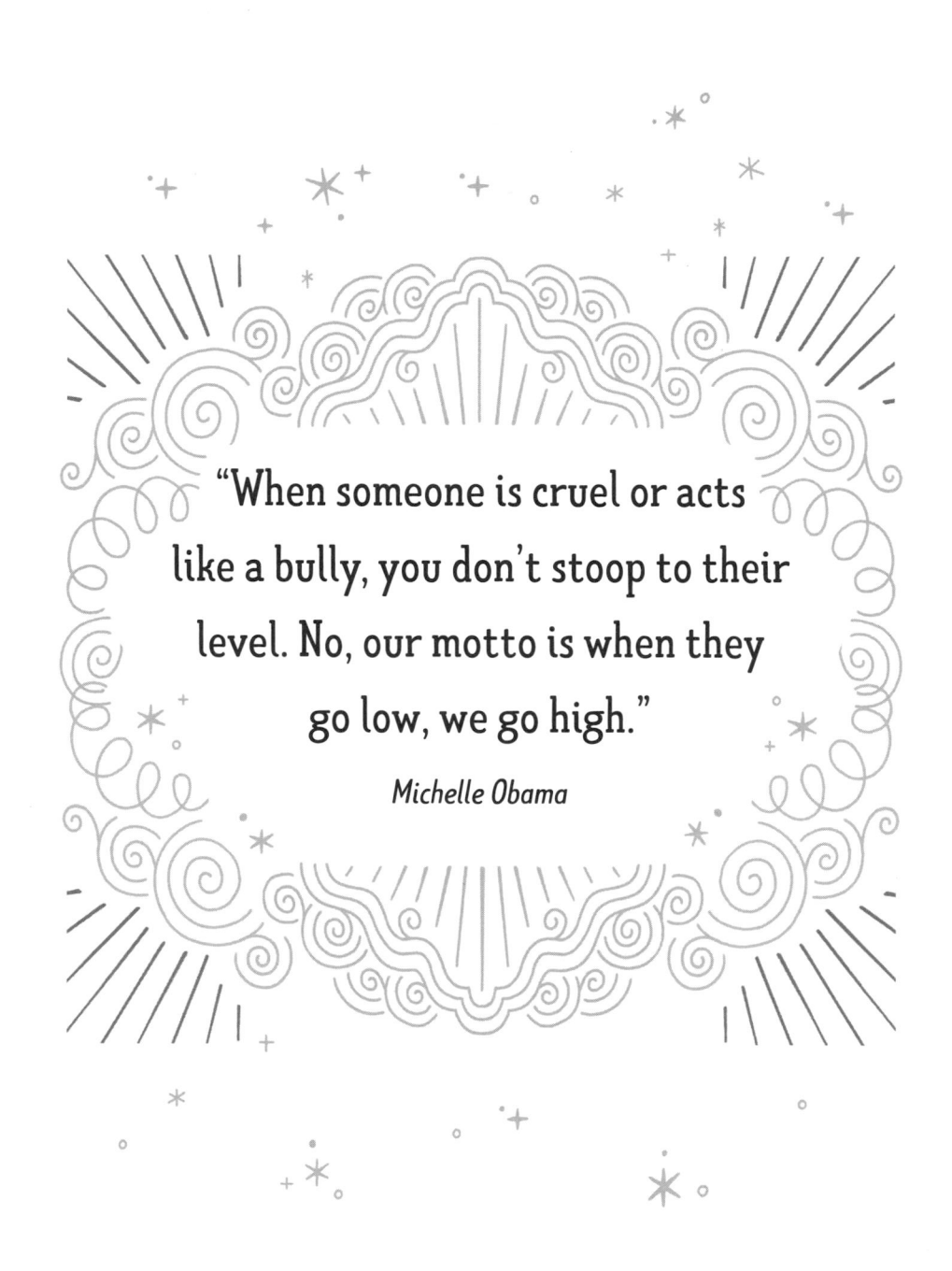

"When someone is cruel or acts
like a bully, you don't stoop to their
level. No, our motto is when they
go low, we go high."

*Michelle Obama*

# YOU'RE IN A SAFE PLACE

**W**ant to know what's awesome about this book? You're holding the key to a secret treasure box of knowledge. This book will empower you to make wise decisions when it comes to one of the toughest issues girls face today: bullying.

It's hard to be in an environment where bullying is happening. As a school counselor, I hear about so many feelings that girls like you experience as they struggle with being bullied. School counselors have an amazing job where we get to help girls one-on-one find their voice and stop patterns of bullying. Today, I want to help empower you to find your voice. Once you learn the secrets in this book, you can apply them to your life right away and fill up your treasure box.

I wrote this book to really encourage you to find your own voice. This is your private space to reflect and respond openly about your struggles with bullying. Go through it with an open mind and heart. Showing care and kindness to yourself is the first step in showing them to others.

Learning more about bullying gives you a special power. It puts you in a special position to help others. You'll learn to look at why girls can become mean. You will also learn how to walk away from the bully and end the conversation on a healthy note. This will show your friends and schoolmates how to overcome bullying in a healthy way, too. Congratulations on taking this big step forward!

Keep adding these skills to the treasure chest that's meant for only you. This treasure chest will help you lead a happy and healthy life, even as you get older. The more you know these skills and practice using them, the more confident you will be.

# HOW TO USE THIS BOOK

This book is meant to be a safe place for you to record your thoughts and emotions. It includes quizzes, charts, and places to write and reflect. Use the activities in this resource to respond openly. If you have questions, jot them out to the side in the margin. Feel free to use this book as your own personal bully-busting diary. If you have questions along the way, make sure you reach out to an adult you trust—a family member, a school counselor, a teacher, or someone else who will listen and help you navigate your situation. Discussing these things with them can give you extra support you may need.

Before we jump in, I want to tell you that I'm so proud of you! You've already made progress just by picking up this book. You're making such a wise decision to address the bullying in your own life and gain awareness for others who may be having a hard time too. As you're reading, think about your own experiences and feel free to make connections to the text. Also take time to think about how it would feel to be in situations like this if you haven't experienced them.

# CHAPTER 1

# WHAT IS BULLYING?

**D**oes it sometimes feel like bullying is everywhere and that you won't be able to avoid it? Bullying can cause a lot of pain and frustration because it can seem so complicated and confusing. The good news is that you don't have to feel this way. You have the right to feel safe, secure, and confident. Surrounding yourself with people and situations that make you feel good and support you is extremely important. This book is here to help clear up the confusion and make things a lot less complicated. So much can be done to battle bullying, and the first step is understanding it.

# Breaking Down Bullying

Bullying is when someone uses their words and actions to try to control you or the situation. It can cause hurt feelings and make you feel rejected and ashamed. Acts of bullying can look different for a lot of people, but it all comes down to power and control. Some kids think that the way to be liked by others is to have more power, because it means they can influence people's choices. You can probably think of some girls who seem to have that influence. But while some girls have an amazing ability to use their influence for good and do positive things, others use their influence to control people. This aggressive power and control battle is called bullying.

Mean behaviors can start when you're very young. For girls your age, that could look like not including certain people on the playground. Then it can grow over time, and by the time girls reach middle school, these mean behaviors can evolve into backstabbing and manipulating others. When someone is trying to steal your power and control repeatedly—to hurt you either physically or emotionally—they are bullying you.

Let's look at an example. Sasha is sitting alone on a bench outside school. Two older girls walk by, giving Sasha dirty looks and whispering secrets about her. Her classmate, Reena, is nearby and sees what is happening. Reena decides to sit with Sasha to check in on how she's doing. Sasha says she feels hurt and left out.

Because this has never happened to her before, she didn't know how to respond to the girls. She felt helpless. To help Sasha feel better, Reena asks to go on a walk together, away from the older girls.

In this example, can you pick out the key parts that make this mean behavior? Yes, the two older girls are trying to gain power over your friend, and there are also signs they are trying to emotionally hurt her. But the key element here is that it's the first time this has happened to her. Bullying is repeated unkind behaviors, so if the older girls continue to do this every time they see her, it's bullying.

Is this type of behavior okay? Absolutely not! Reena did an amazing thing out of empathy for Sasha. Reena saw how she could be feeling and acted out of compassion to join her. This is what girls need more of: kindness, empathy, and compassion. Rise up to the challenge the next time you see a friend struggling.

# Bullying Facts and You

Check all the boxes that apply to things you've experienced:

☐ One in five tweens (9 to 12 years old) say they have been cyberbullied (or bullied online), cyberbullied others, or seen cyberbullying.

☐ One out of every five students says they have been bullied.

☐ Nearly one in eight students being bullied says they were made fun of, called names, or insulted.

☐ Seventy percent of tweens say they have tried to help someone being bullied at school.

☐ Almost one-third of students who were bullied say it affected their friendships.

☐ Nearly 70 percent of students say bullying made them have negative feelings about themselves.

☐ Forty-four percent of kids being bullied say they think it's because of how they look.

☐ More than half of bullying situations stop because a peer helped the student being bullied.

- [ ] More than half of the students (12 to 18 years old) who were bullied say the bully was able to influence what other kids thought about them.

- [ ] Three out of four students said they used the strategy of pretending like it didn't bother them.

- [ ] Of those students who reported being bullied, 13 percent were made fun of or called names. Another 13 percent were the subject of rumors and 5 percent were pushed or shoved. Five percent said they were excluded from activities on purpose.

- [ ] Students who have been bullied were twice as likely to feel physically upset, which included headaches and stomachaches.

- [ ] Tweens reported using a variety of strategies to stop bullying. They include blocking the person bullying them (60 percent), telling a parent (51 percent), ignoring the person (43 percent), reporting it to the website or app (30 percent), and taking a break from the device (30 percent).

# Why Do People Bully?

There is no exact answer or specific reason why people bully. Kids are unique and have a lot of factors that make up who they are. People have different personalities and life experiences that determine the choices they make and the way they behave. Most of the time when kids feel valued, heard, and supported, they're less likely to feel the need to bully or to take someone else's power and control. There are several areas to look at when it comes to why kids bully.

A global youth charity called Ditch the Label did a study to find characteristics of why people bully. They were able to narrow it down to five factors:

1. They are experiencing stress and trauma.

2. They've been taught to respond with aggressive behaviors.

3. They have low self-esteem.

4. They are being bullied themselves.

5. They have a difficult home situation.

This study shows that negative life experiences and relationships can impact someone's choice to bully. So if someone is bullying you, take a closer a look at other factors that might explain why she is doing it.

Think about the following scenario:

Frankie's mom and dad separated when she was nine years old. The adjustment caused her to feel very lonely and frustrated. Over the first couple months, she developed some unpleasant ways to deal with things. In fact, at soccer practice, Frankie's behavior became mean toward a teammate who plays the same position.

In this example, Frankie is experiencing some trauma and stress because of her parents' separation. Instead of working through those feelings in a positive way and relieving some of the stress, Frankie is building negative ways to cope. We can see from this situation that Frankie is experiencing at least three of the five factors: stress and trauma, a difficult home situation, and insecure relationships. Looking at Frankie's whole situation can allow the adults and friends in her life to give her support.

## Bullying Versus Teasing

Not every mean thing kids do will be considered bullying—there's a fine line between bullying and teasing. In fact, kids can be downright mean sometimes, but that might not be all it takes to label them a bully. Usually, there must be at least three things to make a behavior fit into bullying territory. First, there needs to be an imbalance of power. For example, someone bigger and older who has more social status might target someone they see as weaker. Second, the mean behavior is consistently repeated—it's not just a one-time thing, and you feel like the person is mean to you all the time.

Last, you feel like this person is going to hurt you physically, emotionally, or verbally.

Being mean is not bullying. This statement is bland, but it's true. We need to make sure we are labeling bullying for what it is. If girls label every mean thing another girl does to them as bullying, others will begin to think it's not very important. Schools see this all the time because kids will label something as bullying when it's really mean behavior. There is no excuse for mean behavior, and it shouldn't happen anywhere—especially in the school environment, which should be inviting and safe. Reporting mean behavior for what it is will help distinguish what is and isn't bullying.

Throughout this book, you will learn strategies to overcome some of these behaviors and to distinguish between what is mean and what is bullying. Remember, when you feel like it crosses the line and has all three bully components, please tell a trusted adult. Along with your newly learned strategies from this book, adults can give you extra support you may need. Regardless, you have power in your voice—don't be afraid to use it.

# CHECKING IN

It's time to check in with yourself and how you feel about what you've learned. Think about a time when you witnessed a student bully another student. Why do you think the bully lashed out at the other person? What did that teach you about healthy communication?

-----------------------------------------

-----------------------------------------

-----------------------------------------

-----------------------------------------

-----------------------------------------

-----------------------------------------

-----------------------------------------

-----------------------------------------

-----------------------------------------

-----------------------------------------

-----------------------------------------

# True or False: Is This Bullying?

1. Bullying is part of growing up. **True / False**

2. Girls usually bully others physically. **True / False**

3. Someone who bullies may not be aware of their own negative emotions. **True / False**

4. Spreading gossip and rumors can be just as hurtful as hurting someone physically. **True / False**

5. Telling a trusted adult can be the best way to stop the bullying. **True / False**

6. Everyone can tell when someone is being bullied. **True / False**

7. Bullying happens when no one is around. **True / False**

8. Cyberbullying is a growing concern. **True / False**

9. Having a stomachache, headache, and/or anxious thoughts can be related to bullying. **True / False**

10. Fighting back is the only way to make bullying stop. **True / False**

1. False 2. False 3. True 4. True 5. True 6. False 7. False 8. True 9. True 10. False

# WHAT IS BULLYING?

Now that you're diving into what bullying is, let's explore more of what you see at school and beyond. Write in the lines below.

**Cyberbullying** _____
_____
_____

**Emotional** _____
_____
_____

**Verbal** _____
_____
_____

**Hazing** _____
_____
_____

**Gossip** _____
_____
_____

**Physical** _____
_____

# Girls Can Be Mean

Often, we view girl bullying differently than we do boy bullying—and there's good reason for that. Research tells us that girls who bully do it with their relationships. This is called relational aggression, and it's the secrets, rumors, dirty looks, and exclusion that make other girls feel bad. Boys, on the other hand, tend to bully physically with pushing and shoving. This doesn't mean that girls won't physically bully or that boys won't spread rumors, but, overall, there are some differences when it comes to bullying and gender.

Girls who bully often do it secretly, so it's hard for others to see that bullying is happening. In a study by the National Center for Education Statistics, girls who reported bullying at school said they were mostly bullied in the hallway, stairwell, bathroom, or cafeteria. During the school day, this can make it hard for others—including adults—to see what is happening. Don't be afraid to speak up for yourself or a friend.

Expectations play a role in this, too, which doesn't help bullying behavior. Have you noticed that the world around us has views on how we should act and look? Girls are usually taught through social expectations that they should be nice, gentle, passive, thin, beautiful, smart, and so on. This is a lot to think about, let alone try to live up to every day. Not only is it completely exhausting, but it couldn't be further from the truth.

The truth is, girls are unique and have the right to be bold, different, and valued for who they are.

Bullying can happen because of these expectations. There are girls who are amazingly unique and different who break free from these social norms. The old saying "You are your looks" has got to go! So much negativity and body shaming can happen from saying and believing a statement like that. It invites bullying behavior and suggests that anyone not fitting into this body image mold shouldn't be included. Your looks do not define who you are. You are not on this earth to fit into other people's molds. Define yourself for who you are and understand the amazing purpose you have.

Take a stand today and be ready to shine your light. Be daring and bold. Show kindness through your smile and unite with other girls to stop bullying. You have a voice and the right to use it. In fact, our individual experiences are what make the world diverse and beautiful. Look around you—no one person is exactly like another. There are tons of different looks, talents, interests, and personalities. Each one of them is just as valuable as the next.

## Bullying and Body Boundaries

Make no mistake, all bullying hurts emotionally and can have a long-lasting impact. But there is one common form of cyberbullying that can cause a lot of negative effects. This is a type of emotional bullying called body shaming—when someone makes judgmental comments about the size, shape, or appearance of a person's body. This is not okay. In fact, according to a study by the Child Advocacy Center of Lapeer County from Oakland University, 47 percent of girls ages 11 to 21 said the way they look holds them back and limits what they can do. In a nutshell, girls are saying that they feel they are not capable of doing big things because of their looks. Girls, if you hear anything in this book, let it be this: You are undoubtedly amazing, and you are made to do big things! The world needs girls just like you to do the extraordinary! Don't let others carry the power and hold you back from using your potential. What you are capable of has nothing to do with your body image.

Self-respect is one of the best ways to show others that you're confident and love yourself for who you are. Respecting yourself is where you understand your boundaries, physically and emotionally. It's like having your own secret security system with invisible laser beams. If someone crosses it, you immediately recognize something isn't right, and you have the confidence to say so. Building self-respect and confidence can take time, so make sure to practice every day. Do things that boost your confidence and make your heart happy. Some girls like to draw, sing, dance, or write. These are great stress relievers and fun ways to build your hidden talents.

It's also helpful to find other girls who enjoy the same things you do so that you understand that you don't have to change your interests just to fit in. Surround yourself with people who embrace your differences and like you for who you are. You are awesome just the way you are, and believe me, there are other girls out there who would love to do these fun things with you. Setting healthy boundaries and being true to yourself will benefit you for the rest of your life.

## Unity Is Cool

Do you know how it feels to be a part of something bigger than yourself? Maybe you've been part of a sports team or acted in a play. Being together with others brings a feeling of unity. It helps us feel connected in a way where we feel supported, valued, and respected. In other words, it makes us feel like we have friends who have our backs when things get tough. Every single person—boys, girls, older, younger—can benefit from unity. Things are better when we are connected.

How do you show unity? One way is to build empathy. That's where you can see yourself in someone else's shoes and you understand what it would feel like to experience those feelings. For example, one day you watch as your friend gets on the bus. She doesn't talk to anyone and slumps down into the seat. Suddenly you see a tear sliding down her cheek. You probably know how she's feeling, right? Understanding how someone is feeling because you've experienced something similar is called empathy.

In this situation, what do you do? When you decide to do something with those empathy feelings and act on the situation, it turns into compassion. Go sit by your friend or talk to her when you're getting off the bus. Tell her you noticed how sad she looked this morning and ask if there's anything you can do to help. Showing others compassion builds connection. Isn't it cool that you have the power to build connection with others just by what you choose to do?

In fact, there's a whole day set aside for students to recognize how important it is to build connection. Unity Day is a nationally recognized day celebrated by kids in October of every year. The purpose of Unity Day is to build kindness, acceptance, and inclusion. Each step you take to stand with others is an enormously powerful one, and you can do your part by starting now. You have the power to control your choices. Decide to sit with someone new at lunch or invite them to your table to get to know them more. Also try saying "hi" to people outside your friend circle. Once you start doing it, you can become an influence for others, and a ripple effect will begin to happen.

# Express Yourself

1. Find a mirror and look at yourself. The first step to building confidence and practicing self-care is believing these things to be true. Try saying at least five compliments, and then write down what you said. How did it feel to look at yourself and say such positive things?

------------------------------------------------

------------------------------------------------

------------------------------------------------

------------------------------------------------

------------------------------------------------

2. What are some of your go-to self-care activities? Some girls enjoy singing, drawing, dancing, listening to music, and so on. Spend some time writing about your favorite things to do.

------------------------------------------------

------------------------------------------------

------------------------------------------------

------------------------------------------------

------------------------------------------------

# CHECKING IN

It's time to check in with yourself and how you feel about what you've learned. Think about your own experiences. Write your thoughts here.

---------------------------------------------------------------

---------------------------------------------------------------

---------------------------------------------------------------

---------------------------------------------------------------

---------------------------------------------------------------

---------------------------------------------------------------

---------------------------------------------------------------

---------------------------------------------------------------

---------------------------------------------------------------

---------------------------------------------------------------

---------------------------------------------------------------

---------------------------------------------------------------

---------------------------------------------------------------

# CHAPTER 2

# THE MANY FACES OF BULLIES

Bullying takes many forms and can happen in various places. Some girls experience bullying at school, online, and even at home with their friends. In this chapter, you'll learn about common types of bullying and gather the tools you need to combat these different forms. We'll discuss sensitive topics that might stir up some strong emotions, but you'll also learn how to protect yourself from bullying behavior and how to release some of the strong feelings you may be facing.

# Words Hurt

You've probably heard the saying "Sticks and stones may break my bones, but words will never hurt me." Kids say this to help them feel more in control when someone is calling them names, but it doesn't always work. Instead, they might think they're weak because the words did hurt. Verbal bullying is when a person uses spoken language to gain power over their peers— put-downs, insults, name-calling, tormenting, and so on. It's a very common form of bullying.

How can you tell when someone is verbally bullying? Mean behaviors involving name-calling and insults are never okay. Unfortunately, kids use put-downs so often that it can feel like a normal part of growing up—but it's not. Everyone has the right to be treated with respect. Verbal bullying can start off with seemingly harmless and silly teasing, but there's a fine line. When you feel the situation escalating and/or happening repeatedly, it's probably crossing into bullying territory.

Think about how you're feeling when things like this happen. If you feel happy and you're having fun with your friends, that's okay. But take time to listen to your gut feeling. If it's telling you that your friend is taking it too far, you can ask them to stop. And if you're the one teasing, remember your empathy skills—try to recognize how your friends are feeling while you're "playing around." If you see it hurt their feelings, be quick to say you're sorry.

Eleanor Roosevelt said, "No one can make you feel inferior without your consent." This statement is hard but true. Your value and worth aren't based on what other people think of you, so don't give others permission to put you down and make you feel inferior. All girls should have equal power with one another. No one person carries all the power. Take time to grow and strengthen your confidence and the way you see yourself.

## Strengthening Your Shield

Imagine you're going into battle with a shield of protection. The stronger your shield is, the better you'll be at winning this battle against bullying. There are a few different shields you can use.

### Assertiveness

Start using your assertiveness skills by telling people to stop when you don't like what they're doing. This isn't being mean or rude—you have the right to say no. You might think you're too shy to be assertive, but you can build up to it. Look in the mirror, find your "I mean business" voice, and practice telling the other person to stop.

### Attitude

Using your attitude to brush things off can be another way to strengthen your shield when you're in a situation like this. Valuing yourself and not believing what they say to be true will be one of the keys to using this strategy. Try to build your self-talk with positives instead of negatives. This will help strengthen your confidence and the way you see yourself.

### Walking Away

Another way to get out of bullying behavior is to walk away from the situation. Of course, this may not be a long-term fix, but in the moment, you don't want the behavior to get worse. When you can, surround yourself with other people, such as your friends and teachers. The closer you are to your support network, the better off you'll be.

## When It's More Than Words

Bullying often happens over time. The person bullying you can get angrier, things can escalate, and they may move to the next form of hurtful behavior. Kids who reported cyberbullying often said they were physically bullied as well. But is it ever okay to fight back? According to one study, students reported that hitting, fighting, and making plans to get back at the bully only made things worse. In fact, these same students said that telling their friends or an adult at home about the situation was the most helpful thing they did. You have a right to protect yourself, but initiating fights to get even is not the answer.

Being smart about using your tools can help you fight back the right way. Using your voice for good is the most powerful weapon you have, and you're not tattling by reporting bullying behavior. Tell as many adults as you can about what's going on—your parents, teachers, school counselor, and so on—because the more eyes that are on you, the more support you'll have throughout the day. Spending time with friends talking about what's happening and helping one another out of hurtful situations can also make things better. There is power in numbers. That doesn't mean you necessarily need someone else to take care of the situation for you, but having people who support you helps build your confidence to resolve it.

"If everything was perfect, you would never learn and you would never grow."

*Beyoncé*

Try these five quick tips to stop verbal bullies in their tracks.

1.  **Stay calm.** This helps your brain decide what you're going to do next.

2.  **Get support.** Tell others what's been happening so they can support you and help intervene when needed.

3.  **Be assertive.** Use your "I mean business" voice and tell the other person to stop. You don't have to stick around and give them a long reason why. Just let them know.

4.  **Practice positive self-talk.** Remember you're valued and what they're saying isn't true. Keep feeding yourself positive messages.

5.  **Walk away.** Confidently walk away and get into activities that make you happy.

# Emotional Scars

When someone is targeting your emotions and trying to destroy your positive character, it's called emotional bullying. Girls may do this through ignoring or excluding someone from a group, humiliating others, ganging up against someone, or using sarcasm to make someone feel small.

Emotional bullying is a roller coaster that can leave lifelong impacts and result in permanent emotional scars. When girls experience emotional bullying, they often start to feel embarrassed because they are being made to feel less than. But the thing is, usually the person who is emotionally bullying them is doing it to lots of different people because it makes them feel powerful and like they have more control. In other words, the point of their emotional bullying is to make you lose control over your emotions. The person doing the bullying wants you to believe that you're worthless so that they feel like they are better than you. But it's not true—don't believe the lies!

Kids have funny sayings for everything. Have you heard the one that goes, "I'm rubber, you're glue, whatever you say bounces off me and sticks to you"? It's been around for a long time, but it's still relevant today, especially when it comes to emotional bullying. Rubber is thick and bouncy, so creating a thick skin like rubber can help bounce off some of the negative words that may come your way.

Remember, you are amazing just the way you are. Your personality and interests are what make you special and unique. The world needs you to be you! Try to gain a new perspective and shift your point of view. If someone is attacking your emotions and self-worth, try not to take it personally and instead remember that it's more a reflection of them and how they are feeling. To keep your mind off it, stay connected to your interests and what makes you happy, whether you play sports, dance, sing, paint, act, or write. Keep doing what makes you feel loved, valued, and confident. You don't have to invite people who can't see your goodness and value into your life. You get to decide who your friends are, so make them count. Try to surround yourself only with people who make you feel good about yourself.

## Bullying and Identity

There's a particular form of bullying, known as identity-based bullying, that targets the core of who someone is as a person. This form of bullying can be sensitive to talk about because it doesn't just affect girls physically or emotionally. It targets a person's race, gender, sexual orientation, or any other aspect of identity. This form of bullying is targeted at groups of people or individuals based on the personal bias or prejudice of the person bullying. Prejudice is when someone forms an opinion that isn't based on facts or actual experiences. One example of this would be a bully who is making fun of a student for using her hands to speak because she is deaf. They are being mean not because the girl is deaf but because the person bullying has bias or an opinion that the girl is not as smart as them. Do you see the difference that biases can make?

This is important to learn about and take time to reflect on. If you've experienced something like this or if you've created some unfair biases about other people yourself, think about that now. Do you know groups of people or individuals who are targeted more than others based on their identity?

Everyone has a right to be who they are without judgment from other people. Your social groups should be respectful and inclusive. Girls need each other, so practice being an ally and get to know others instead of being judgmental. Wouldn't it be exciting to have a wide variety of differences in your social group? What a great learning experience!

## Asking for Help

If you are being bullied or feel like you are the one bullying, talk to an adult you trust about it. Tell your parents or another adult family member what has been going on. They can support you and get you the help you need. In rare situations, there might be adults who won't be able to help, but that's okay—find someone else to tell. Keep going to the next person until someone can connect you with the help you need. Usually, adults at school are trained to help in these situations. Go to your teacher, counselor, and/or principal to get school support.

When should you tell someone?

- You feel like you've been the victim of any type of bullying.

- You've tried to make it stop, and it's not getting better.

- You feel excluded, embarrassed, and hurt by other people's actions or comments.

- You feel disrespected and judged because of who you are.

How should you start this conversation?

- Find an adult you trust who will talk through this with you and actively listen to your concerns.

- Tell them you need help with a problem you can't handle on your own. Be firm in stating that you want this to stop.

- Be ready to share what you have tried and what the results were.

- Ask for advice on what can be done next to help you feel safe, valued, and supported.

Signs you might be bullying someone else:

- You feel like people get upset with you easily.

- You think it's funny to call out the mistakes or insecurities of others.

- You talk about others behind their back.

- You feel like you don't have true friends.

Going to an adult for help is not a sign of weakness. It's a very brave thing to do. Have courage to tell an adult when something is out of your control. You don't have to face bullying alone, even if you feel like you have been the one doing the bullying behavior.

# Remember and Release

1. First, write about a time when you were bullied. Recall as much as you can about the situation.

   ------------------------------------------------

   ------------------------------------------------

   ------------------------------------------------

   ------------------------------------------------

   ------------------------------------------------

   ------------------------------------------------

   ------------------------------------------------

   ------------------------------------------------

   ------------------------------------------------

2. Now we are going to practice releasing the feelings that are attached to the situation. Imagine blowing up a balloon. With every breath, fill up the balloon with your bullying experience. It's like you're trapping it in the balloon and it gets bigger with every breath, in the same way the feelings grow when you think about your experience.

3. Once the imaginary balloon is full of your experience, tie it off and let it go. Breathe slowly as you watch your balloon go higher and higher until you can't see it anymore. It's completely gone. When you're finished, write about how you're feeling now that you've released your balloon.

-------------------------------------------

-------------------------------------------

-------------------------------------------

-------------------------------------------

-------------------------------------------

-------------------------------------------

-------------------------------------------

-------------------------------------------

-------------------------------------------

-------------------------------------------

-------------------------------------------

-------------------------------------------

# Online Bullying

Tweens and teens have the computer and internet at their fingertips, so it's not surprising that cyberbullying is all too common among girls those ages. Cyberbullying is when someone uses technology—such as computers, cell phones, and other electronic devices—as a way to harm someone else. It often appears as hurtful social media posts; mean statements made while gaming; hate accounts created to embarrass, threaten, or abuse; or similar forms of cruelty and meanness online. Girls of all ages experience some form of bullying behavior online. In fact:

- Nine out of 10 tweens use social media or gaming apps.

- Twenty percent of tweens have been cyberbullied, have cyberbullied others, or have witnessed cyberbullying.

- When students are victims of cyberbullying, they are usually being bullied in person as well.

- More than half of kids being bullied said the cause of the bullying was due to their appearance.

Many girls face struggles being online, but you can learn tools to help you cope with cyberbullying. While you might feel upset and stuck at first, there's always something that can improve the situation. Filling up your toolkit and strengthening your shield is the first step.

Ask your parents to help you protect your online accounts and learn how to report mean behavior online. Having a system in place before there's a problem is important. Know how to make your online platforms secure and block specific accounts. Taking a proactive approach can help you feel confident and know the steps to take if negative behaviors come your way.

Another great thing to do is team up with your online sisterhood and groups of trusted friends. Make a pact to have eyes out for one another. Girls can move mountains, especially when they are together. Have your friends watch out for negative and hurtful comments about you and let them know you've got their backs, too. Lead with positive examples and make an online stance for the better. We need girls like you to change the world!

## Hidden Bullies

Some girls see the internet as a place to hide and attack without anyone knowing their identity. But did you know everything you do online leaves a digital footprint? It's like digital evidence that can lead back to the person doing it.

Always remember that what you post online never actually goes away, even if it's deleted. This creates a horrible experience for the girls being attacked because they don't know where it's coming from and it may be difficult to make it quickly go away. If you find yourself in this situation, block the person making cruel comments, even if you don't know who they are. Also report the behavior to a trusted adult who can help you navigate the next steps.

Online behavior like this is wrong. You have the right to feel just as safe online as you do at home and at school and in your community. The moment girls sign up for online accounts, they are deciding to leave a digital footprint. Every account that's created (real or fake), every picture and video that's posted, and every comment that's shared will be available. Girls have power, so use your digital footprint for good and make a positive impact online.

## It's Okay to Unplug

In today's digital world, being online seems like it's the connection to everything. In a lot of ways that's true, but you don't have to be connected all the time. There's a time and place to get offline and take breaks from your emails and social media accounts. Creating routines where you can take time offline is important for your mental health. These routines are part of self-care, and they don't have to be fancy—in fact, the simpler they are, the more you will stick to them. Some examples would be not having your phone with you while you're eating, turning off notifications during certain times of the day, and making an effort to put your phone away while you're hanging out with friends and family.

Taking longer breaks is okay, too—there are many influencers and stars who take breaks from social media for longer periods of time. Being connected may seem like you're "in the know" and staying up to date, but some girls find themselves anxious because of too much online information. It's okay to put your phone down and be involved with what's going on in the room. Take time to unplug and recharge.

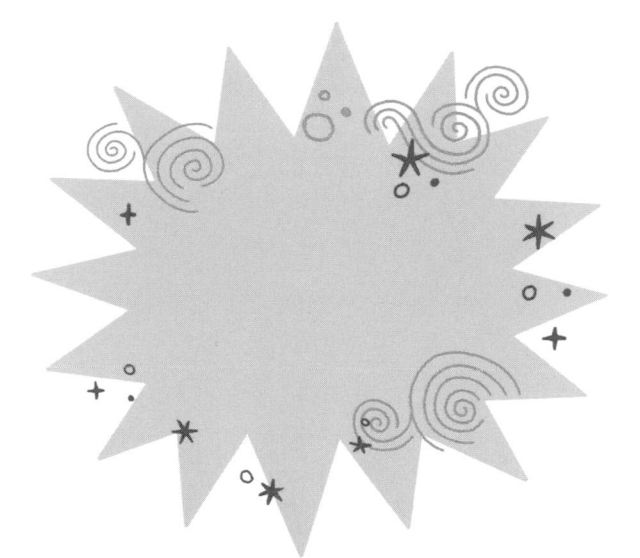

# SEEING HER

Charlie was new to social media, and she decided to create an account with her parents' permission. She was so excited to finally get to use it, until the day some of her classmates shared a hurtful video talking badly about her. She was used to this at school where the other girls often left her out. But this hurt worse. Who else saw this video? She immediately had a gut-wrenching feeling, wondering if everyone felt that same way about her. After talking it through with her best friend and her parents, she was able to put those worries aside. She decided to block the bullies and not believe their lies.

Have you experienced something like Charlie? How did you handle it?

-------------------------------------------------

-------------------------------------------------

-------------------------------------------------

-------------------------------------------------

-------------------------------------------------

# CHAPTER 3

# RESILIENT YOU

Being resilient means you can pick up and keep moving forward. It's being able to stand amid a big storm and then adjust easily when it's all over. When it comes to being affected by bullying, a resilient girl is one who carries on with her life, staying positive and enjoying the things she always has.

Do you want to know the secret to anti-bullying? Each person has the power to decide how they respond and where they want to focus their energy. The person bullying isn't the one in control—you are. So focus on the friendships you want to nurture and grow. This chapter will help you build resilience and find the secret power within.

# Keeping Your Cool

Self-care is taking the time to make sure you're okay so you can stay cool, calm, and collected. If you find yourself in a situation where you need to keep your cool, there are a few tools to help you out.

**Do a quick body scan.** In the heat of the moment, doing a quick internal "check" can help make sure your brain and body are on the same page and can communicate with each other. Your body gives clues to how your brain is reacting. If you scan your body looking for these clues, you might find sweaty palms, clenched fists, red and hot cheeks, a racing heart, or tears swelling in your eyes. These are all normal reactions to tough situations. Once you spot where your big emotions are coming from in your body, try some of the next tricks to keep yourself calm.

Feel each of your five senses. If you find your heart is pounding, or your body really tense, check in with your senses. Hear what sounds are coming into your ears. Notice what smell surrounds you. Let your fingers feel the fabric of your shirt or pants. Doing this can help you refocus your mind and talk with a more calm voice.

**Set a timer.** Walk away for a couple minutes and try to not respond to the situation right away. Look at a clock, your watch, or your phone, note the time, and then set a limit for two minutes. Cool your emotions down by doing the next few things before you go back.

**Focus on your breathing.** When faced with a tough situation, you could very likely benefit from some deep breaths. If you take at least three deep breaths, you will notice your heart rate start to slow down. This is fantastic news if you're wanting to remain calm and let your brain do the talking. One of the easiest ways to do this is to breathe in deeply and slowly to the count of four and let it out slowly to the count of four. Take a moment and practice right now. Inhale, one . . . two . . . three . . . four. Exhale, one . . . two . . . three . . . four. Keep going! Think about how your body feels when you're all done.

**Use your imagination.** Take a second to let your mind visualize yourself being calm and confident. What would you look and sound like if you remained calm?

**Role-play with confidence.** Practicing what you're going to say and how you're going to present yourself will be a great way to ward off any unwanted negative emotions. Grab a friend, sibling, or parent and role-play the situation. Let them know the problem you're facing and ask them to help you come up with what to say.

# Creative Problem-Solving

Getting creative can help you out of a sticky situation. Knowing when to use the right tools and how to go about it can stop a tough situation from getting worse. It's also a good idea to be prepared so you're not caught off guard. In this section, we're going to talk about a few tips and tricks you can use to solve some of these problems.

## Humor

Using humor is a helpful tactic when you're face-to-face with a bully. It's a great way to make light of a heavy situation. First, try to stay positive and not let the bully's comments tear down who you are. Also, don't say funny things that are directed at the person bullying or make it seem like you're making fun of them. The bottom line is, don't believe the negative things the other person is saying and try to turn things around for the better. It's usually best to just walk away after giving one or two funny remarks.

## Body Language

Did you know you can communicate without talking? You definitely can! And it can be a useful strategy when it comes to avoiding bullying behavior. Body language is communicating through our actions and movements. Practicing your body language to communicate confidence can help keep bullying behavior away. Remember, bullying is trying to gain power and control over someone else. That's why your confident body language can deter a bully from trying to tear you down. Practice keeping your shoulders back and your head held high. Look people in the eye when you pass them in the hallway. Go further by giving them a smile and a quick hello. This makes you look confident and shows you are ready to handle anything.

## Friendship

One idea you might not have considered is trying to make friends with the person bullying. Making friends can be tough and might not always be the right solution, so scope it out and see if your bullying scenario could benefit from friendship. It's also best to try this particular tactic with the help of other good friends and not by yourself. Try to include the girl who is bullying by inviting her to play in your group's game, or have the courage to ask her to talk and try to work things out.

# Bully-Busting Plan

There's an older boy on your bus who purposely bumps into you when he walks by. This happens almost every day and makes you feel embarrassed. What could you do to show him that this is not okay without starting a fight? Write down your response.

--------------------------------------------

--------------------------------------------

--------------------------------------------

--------------------------------------------

--------------------------------------------

At recess, two girls sit alongside the fence. Every day, you overhear them saying rude things about their classmates. Today, you hear them talking about you. What can you do to make this stop, for you and other girls they may be talking about? Write down your response.

--------------------------------------------

--------------------------------------------

--------------------------------------------

--------------------------------------------

# The Power of Gratitude

Being thankful is what gratitude is all about. You always have the power to look at things with a fresh perspective and decide to be thankful for what you have. Consider things you love about your life and who you are as a person. Doing this can help you have a greater sense of control over anyone who tries to make you feel differently. The world might not ever be 100 percent bully-free. But you get to decide whether you want to have a fresh perspective and stay positive or keep your attention on the negative bullying behavior.

Creating a gratitude journal can be one way to develop this skill. Truth be told, this technique needs a lot of practice, even in your everyday thoughts. The more you practice being thankful, the more you will naturally be more positive and confident. Designing this journal is simple and easy. Grab a notebook and something to write with. Decorate the front of the notebook any way you want. Inside, write "I am grateful for . . ." and then make a list of things that make you thankful. Just quickly jot down whatever comes to mind. You'll soon notice that if you create a routine of doing this each day, you will have an abundance of things to list because you are becoming more aware of the amazing things around you.

Have you ever seen a horse wearing blinders? These silly looking eye covers are meant to block a horse from seeing to the back or the sides. If you think about it, this is exactly what happens when we're faced with a tough situation like bullying. Our blinders immediately go up, and we have trouble seeing past what is happening right in front of us. Through time and practice, you will start to see more clearly.

It can be normal in hard times to focus on the negative only. If you have trouble identifying good things in your life, talk to a trusted friend or grown-up and have them help you. Gratitude can become a habit after you try it for some time.

"Appreciation can make a day —
even change a life. Your willingness to
put it into words is all that is necessary."

*Margaret Cousins*

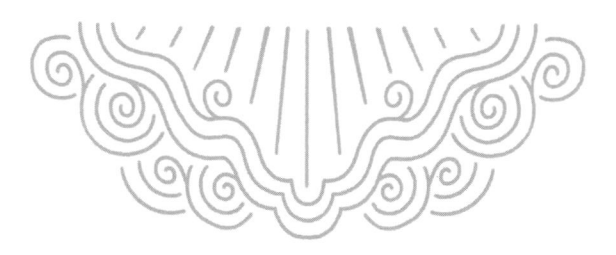

# CHECKING IN

It's time to check in with yourself and how you feel about what you've learned. Think about what gratitude means to you. Is it easy for you to see things in your life that you are grateful for? Write down three of those things here, and list why.

--------------------------------------------------
--------------------------------------------------
--------------------------------------------------
--------------------------------------------------
--------------------------------------------------
--------------------------------------------------
--------------------------------------------------
--------------------------------------------------
--------------------------------------------------
--------------------------------------------------
--------------------------------------------------
--------------------------------------------------
--------------------------------------------------

# 60 Seconds of Being Great

It's time to get started and practice your gratitude skills. Have a clock or timer nearby. Here you will see two writing activities. You will have 30 seconds to create a list for each one.

1.  Set a timer for 30 seconds. Write down all the amazing things you can think of about yourself. Try not to only list physical characteristics. Ready . . . set . . . go!

    ------------------------------------------------

    ------------------------------------------------

    ------------------------------------------------

    ------------------------------------------------

2.  Reset your timer for another 30 seconds. This time, write down all the things you are grateful for in your friends. Think about the characteristics that make them a great friend. Ready . . . set . . . go!

    ------------------------------------------------

    ------------------------------------------------

    ------------------------------------------------

    ------------------------------------------------

# Focus on Yourself

What are things in your life that bring you joy? Thinking about the positives and being able to focus on the good will help you overcome some of these hard situations. Building up resilience will help you throughout your entire life. Shifting the focus inward instead of keeping your eyes on the bullying behavior can help you continue to live a joy-filled life.

Consider the different activities you are involved in. Some girls choose to play sports or get active in other ways like dancing, writing, art, music, and so on. These things can boost your confidence and inspire you to get connected with others who enjoy those things, too. This group of friends can end up being your support network because you might have so much in common. It's a wonderful feeling to have connection and support.

When you're focused on improving something, making things better for others, or getting connected, you end up having little time to worry about things that don't hold a lot of weight or value in your life—such as bullying and others who are putting you down. Let's look at one situation about a girl who decided to shift her mindset.

Alexia used to play volleyball until she realized it wasn't something she enjoyed doing outside school. She showed up at every practice, gave it her all, and after three years decided it didn't bring her joy anymore. Alexia still loved being part of a team, but during recess, some of her old volleyball teammates would play and leave her out. This was frustrating to her because she felt like they should still be close. Instead of trying to include herself during every recess and feeling down because the team was playing without her, she decided to shift her mindset. Over the next few weeks, Alexia got involved with other activities. She joined the junior high choir and started a tutoring club to help younger students in the elementary building. She learned that getting involved with things that make a difference and made her happy, instead of trying to fit in, was a great distraction. She found her talents and used them to make a difference in her life as well as the lives of those around her.

Are there any areas in your life where you need to shift your mindset? Girls of all ages want to belong and feel like they fit in. But it's so important to stay true to who you are and get involved with the right things for you, just like when Alexia decided to shift her mindset when others wouldn't let her play. She could've gotten down and let her negative emotions take over, but she decided to be resilient and focus on what she could do to feel better.

## Staying Positive

When faced with a bullying situation, it can be easy to get down about yourself. In fact, usually that's the goal for the person bullying—they want you to feel bad and want you to hide behind your hurt feelings. Staying positive can be one of the most important things you can do in a situation like this. It helps you stay strong and confident, knowing you are not going to stand down to bullying anymore.

For starters, surround yourself with positive people. Think about your friends who make you feel good and who always have your back. Good friends will continue to fuel your positivity fire. So instead of focusing on negative thoughts such as "No one likes me," try giving your inner voice a pep talk. Tell it that you do have close friends who like you the way you are—and that's better than trying to fit in with everybody anyway.

Another way to stay positive is to avoid engaging with the other person who is being mean. If they're trying to hurt you emotionally, verbally, or even phys-ically, try everything you can to avoid getting into an argument with them. It isn't worth your time. In the heat of the moment, they likely won't be able to see your side clearly and will still be focused on doing you harm or controlling you. It's better to avoid the confrontation and not let your mind be filled with the negative things they're saying to you. Instead, just get away from them.

Being positive and happy can have an influence on others. If you broadcast how happy and positive you are, it can cause a ripple effect among other girls around you. A smile and a simple hello can go a long way. For example, you smile, it causes another girl to smile, and then that smile is passed on to the next girl and the next girl. Remember how, at the beginning of this book, we talked about using your influence for good? This could be one of those situations where it not only helps you feel better, but it can help others, too.

# SELF-SOOTHE AND SELF-EXPRESS

Self-soothing is a way to deal with things that are tough. These are some ways to practice.

1. **Get inspired.** Try listening to music or reading a book.

2. **Get artsy.** Draw, write, or paint!

3. **Get active.** Take care of your body by exercising, dancing, or stretching.

Self-expression is the ability to show others what you're made of. Here are some ideas.

1. **Be a mentor.** Team up with younger students to promote positive change.

2. **Use your talents.** Focus energy on what you're good at and let it inspire you.

3. **Celebrate style.** Get creative and have fun with your outfits and accessories.

What are some ways you self-soothe and express yourself?

# Passion Sauce

Imagine what passion means to you. Being passion-ate about something and being able to share it with others can be a powerful tool. Passion is a strong feeling or emotion that can be a driving force behind some of the choices you make or things you pursue. For example, since you are reading this book about anti-bullying, there must be passion in you that wants to stop mean bullying behavior.

Finding your passions can help you keep focused on the positives in your life. Fueling your energy with things that you're passionate about can help you focus on you, your community, or simply your inter-ests. Girls of all ages need to shift where their focus is and start investing their time and energy into things that really matter to them. If you are clear about your passions, you'll feel more confident in the face of bullying.

Sara is really active in the Green Kids committee at her school, and she loves to be involved and help out her community. But during lunch, Sara is often viewed as an outcast, sitting by herself. She takes this time to read while she's eating instead of socializing. Little do others know, Sara is amazing at writing and drawing. She has also invested her talents by vol-unteering in a community-wide cleanup effort put on by some local businesses, and people see her as an outstanding leader. Sara could look at her lunch situation and start getting sad that no one sits with her or includes her. But instead, she invests her time and energy into what makes her happy. In fact, through this committee, she was able to make friends outside her lunch group and spend time with people who share her passion for the environment.

This is an example of how to find the passion in your own life. You are not defined by the judgments of others, and you have the power to bring light to your hidden talents. Just because some people at school can't see them, that doesn't mean you don't have them. Showcase your talents in other areas of your life—get involved and promote positive change.

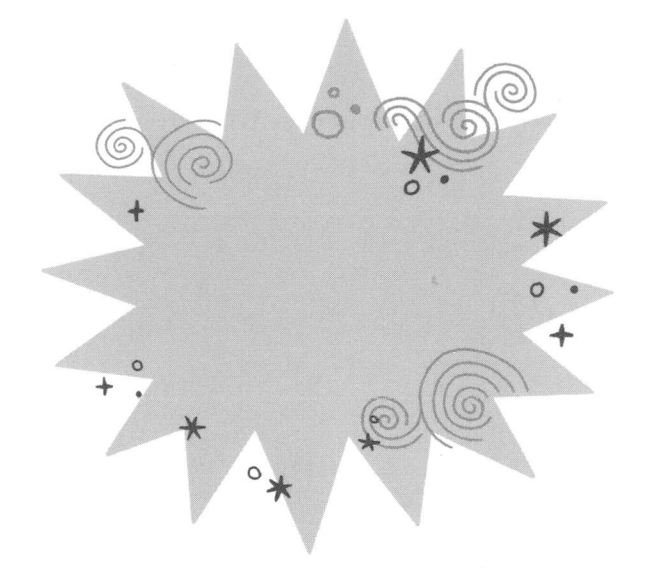

# Passion Project

This activity will help you explore where your interests are and help you brainstorm what you may be passionate about. Grab a piece of paper and a pen!

Start by drawing a circle on the paper. Inside that circle, write the words "I enjoy." From there, draw lines connecting to more bubbles. Inside the new bubbles, write words of things you like. They can be physical things, characteristics, feelings, hobbies, and so on.

Once you have several words spun off your center circle, see where you'd like to keep going and add more detail. There is no right or wrong way to do this.

Take a step back and see what words or phrases jump off the page at you. Color those in with a crayon or colored pencil. Think about how these could become a passion of yours!

# CHAPTER 4

# STANDING UP FOR YOURSELF

S tanding up to bullying behavior doesn't have to be challenging. Decide how you want to handle it and make a powerful plan to stop it in its tracks. You have every right to stand up for yourself and be heard. It takes courage to do hard things like this, but you are more than capable. In this chapter, you will start building your communication skills to speak clearly and assertively. You will also begin to practice using your bravery muscles so that you feel confident and in control when something comes up.

# Speaking Up

It can be extremely hard sometimes to voice your opinion and stand up for yourself. A lot of times, girls like to please others and avoid any confrontation. It's okay to be the nice girl, but there's also a time and place to stand confidently and say, "No, I'm not going to tolerate this." Your voice is your most powerful weapon when it comes to so many life events, not just bullying. It can be used to empathize and relate to people who have been hurt or to include others when they seem left out. Your voice can also be the firm stopping point that makes someone else think about their actions. In this section, you'll discover how the power of your voice can influence the situation, impact the person bullying, and change future bullying outcomes.

Influence—that's a big word, right? It holds a lot of power. That's why bullies like to hold on tightly and try not to let anyone else have it. The power to influence others and get them to see your viewpoint and stand with you can seem overwhelming. But it's not that hard. Girls are amazing at socializing, connecting, and using influence to gain more friends. What's the number one way girls socialize and connect? Through their words. When you're face-to-face with a bully, you still have the power to connect to those around you and influence the situation by what you do or say next. It's an extremely powerful tool. The entire situation can change just by what you say!

You can not only influence the situation and those around you, but you can make an impact on the person bullying, too. By remaining confident, using your voice, and not getting heated, you are showing the person bullying that they don't have to act like this to gain power and control. There's a positive side to influencing—you are setting an example with your words that it's not okay to treat people this way. By remaining confident and in control and showing the person bullying your awesome qualities, you might just influence them enough to change their ways. Maybe not immediately, but over time your words have the power to sink in and allow for self-reflection to happen.

Now, change doesn't always happen for the person bullying, but it's nice when it does. There may come a time when the person bullying stops and you're able to have a good conversation with them. Use your words to explain how hurtful it was to be treated that way and that no one deserves that kind of treatment. Explain how you would like to be friends and work this out. Using your voice to make things better will ultimately create change for other girls around you because they can follow your example, remain confident, and stand up to bullying. No one likes to be attacked or hurt with words, so use them for good and to stand up for what's right.

# 10 Phrases to Get You Started

Here are 10 one-liners that can help stop bullying quickly. Practice saying these out loud to yourself in a mirror while working on your serious face. Make sure you express body language that is confident. Once you're comfortable with that, try role-playing with a friend or an adult.

1. **Stop!** Just shouting "stop" will bring attention to you, which is exactly what you want in a bullying situation. Bystanders will be able to notice what's going on and intervene if needed.

2. **That's not okay!** Let the person doing the bullying know that their behavior is not okay and that they can't treat others like this.

3. **Cut it out—it's not funny!** When teasing crosses the line, it's okay to let the other person know that it went too far. If you never tell them it's wrong, they may continue to do it.

4. **Whatever.** This saying has been around for a while, but it can help quickly change the subject and roll the negativity right off. Immediately let it go and move on!

5. **No one deserves to be treated this way!** It's hard to see another student being treated unfairly, and girls need each other to step in. This saying can be used in the line of fire when another friend needs help.

6. **Leave me alone!** Just like yelling "stop," this statement can draw attention and let the other person know you aren't going to tolerate their behavior anymore.

7. **Hey, that's my friend—quit doing that!** By saying "that's my friend," you are being inclusive and helping the person being bullied feel like they have backup.

8. **Wow, did you think of that all by yourself?** Using humor can be a great deflector when faced with rude and hurtful comments.

9. **You can think what you want, but I'm happy the way I am.** Keeping your confidence and staying positive can be one of bullying's biggest deterrents.

10. **Are you kidding me?** The person doing the bullying wants to see a big reaction out of you. Instead, try this straightforward statement and walk away.

# What's Your Communication Style?

Use this quiz to think about how you communicate and use it to identify the most comfortable way for you to speak up.

**Passive communication** is a style where the person doesn't directly express their feelings, wants, or needs.

**Aggressive communication** is a style where the person expresses things in a hostile manner, even if it violates the rights of others.

**Assertive communication** is a style where the person expresses what they feel, need, or want within the limits of respecting the other person.

**Now you try:** Which communication style fits each of the following statements?

1. I like to get out of everyone's way.

2. I often interrupt others.

3. I state what I want in a nice way.

4. I usually walk with my head down.

5. I apologize all the time.

6. I try not to blame others, and I take responsibility for my actions.

7. I am quick to blame others for their mistakes.

8. I remain respectful but stand up for myself.

9. I try to control the conversation by talking loudly.

10. I stay quiet so that I don't accidentally anger someone with my words.

Talk to an adult about your communication style. If you fall more toward the passive or aggressive communication style, you may want to do some activities to practice your assertive skills.

1, 4, 5, and 10 = Passive
2, 7, and 9 = Aggressive
3, 6, and 8 = Assertive

# CHECKING IN

It's time to check in with yourself and how you feel about what you've learned. Think about your recent year or two in school. In the space below write about a time when one of these statements would have been helpful. Which statement did you pick? Can you see yourself using it in the future?

------------------------------------------------

------------------------------------------------

------------------------------------------------

------------------------------------------------

------------------------------------------------

------------------------------------------------

------------------------------------------------

------------------------------------------------

------------------------------------------------

------------------------------------------------

------------------------------------------------

------------------------------------------------

------------------------------------------------

# Bravery Is a Muscle

Just like bodybuilders work out to gain muscle, you need to give attention to your mental and emotional skills so that they grow stronger. Strengthening your bravery muscle is a lot like pumping iron—it means fueling yourself with the right ingredients to grow courage. One way to do this is through positive self-talk. The more you digest positivity, the better off you'll be at showing confidence and courage. Another way to build your bravery muscle is through consistency. Staying consistent and being brave in tough times can help you grow stronger. If you decided to be brave for only one month and hide out the rest of the school year, your bravery muscle would become weak.

Here are two examples of girls who decided to grow and strengthen their bravery muscles.

Bianca was a happy-go-lucky girl who loved making friends. Over the course of a few weeks, she noticed one of her classmates being rude to some other girls in the locker room after gym class. Bianca disliked how it was making the other girls feel, and she felt in her heart she needed to do something. She decided to let the gym teacher know what was happening in the locker room. Bianca decided to use a subtle way to navigate a sticky situation.

Gia tried to avoid the hallway every day because some girls always hung around her locker and said rude things to her about what she was wearing. Gia felt really uncomfortable around them and didn't think there was anything wrong with what she was wearing. Eventually, Gia decided she'd had enough. She walked up to her locker, took a deep breath, and said, "Stop talking about me!" By this time, all eyes were on Gia, so she continued by saying, "No one likes it when you make fun of them, including me!" Then she turned around and walked away, feeling proud of herself for standing up to the other girls. Gia decided on a bold way to handle the girls at her locker.

Whichever way you decide to do it, using your bravery muscle is okay. Just make sure you're doing it out of what is right and respectful to you and other girls who may need a hand.

# WHEN TO IGNORE IT

Ignoring a person who is bullying may be a powerful tool when used the right way.

Sometimes this strategy allows both parties to cool down and not have a confrontation while they're both upset. But, this can be hard for some. It takes guts to not pay attention to that negative behavior. Once you realize that you have the power to help stop hurtful comments and behaviors, ignoring bullies will become easier.

Bullies want a big reaction, and when you give them nothing, it can help settle things down.

There are times, though, when ignoring a bully can aggravate them and make the situation worse. In that instance, it's best to keep good eye contact, use a calm and even tone of voice, and stand an appropriate distance from the bully.

Ignoring is also a way to continue letting it happen to others, and we don't want that! If you decide to use this tactic, make sure you tell an adult what's going on, too.

When faced with a situation like this, is it more comfortable for you to ignore it or face it head on? Why or why not?

# You've Got This: At School and Beyond

Bullying is not fixed to one place. Sometimes it can seem relentless and be hard to get away from, and it may even feel like it's following you around. But remember that there is always hope and you need to know you aren't alone in this fight against bullying. This book will teach you so many ideas that will help you take control of these situations. Sometimes bullying can be overwhelming and seem like you need someone else to step in—and that's perfectly fine. Tell someone in your life who you trust and who can help you navigate these situations. You deserve to experience life with excitement and joy, knowing you are enough and that you're valued for exactly who you are.

Whether bullying behavior happens at school, during extracurricular activities, or online, there should always be someone who can help support you. Take note of all the things throughout this book that you can do to support yourself, but also gather some adults in your network—teachers, parents, coaches—who could give you backup if you need it. Remember, it isn't a sign of weakness to get help. In fact, it's the total opposite. It shows how brave, confident, and assertive you can be. Battling bullying behavior can be extremely challenging and it can weigh very heavily on you. Just like soldiers support each other when going into battle, you need support, too, even when you feel like you have it all under control.

## Finding Your Groove at School

It can be extremely hard to walk into school and be a student because there are tons of things that make your mind drift off. Sometimes it's challenging to sit in class, listen to your teacher, and keep your focus. Whether the bullying is happening in the schoolyard or class-room, there are ways to keep your focus right where it needs to be—on your learning!

Imagine you're carrying a backpack and you put a rock inside for everything that's on your mind. These rocks can even match the size of the problem you're facing: one rock for soccer practice, one rock for Sammie calling you names, one rock for your mom getting on you for not doing your homework. Now how heavy is your backpack? Is it so full it won't zip? This is one example of why it can be so hard to focus while you're at school. Instead of trying to focus on everything at once, spend some time unpacking your backpack and setting aside each rock. This way, while you're at school, the only thing you need to focus on is your learning.

Another thing you can do in the classroom to focus on learning is to make sure you are organized. This means being prepared for class and having all the supplies you need. Get out your notebook and pencil and take notes. Lean in and actively listen to what your teacher has to say. Being an active participant will not only help you focus, but it will help you soak in the lesson as well.

If bullying behavior keeps happening in the class-room to the point where you can't focus and you've tried unpacking your backpack of thoughts, there are a few more things to try. If you're sitting by the person distracting you, ask the teacher if you can move to another seat. If that doesn't work, try talking to your teacher and explaining the situation. Let them know you're trying to handle it on your own, but you may need someone to check in and see if things are going okay. This gives you the opportunity to try to handle it within your own limits but also gives you the comfort of having an adult there to support you.

If it's still happening, the best thing to do is to tell another adult. Reporting bullying is not a sign of weak-ness—you are being strong for yourself and the other students who may be having this same problem. Go see your school counselor or principal and let them know what's been repeatedly happening and the things you've tried doing to make it stop. You are not alone, and sometimes adults can be the biggest support in stopping bullying behavior.

# Affirmation Station

Affirmations are things you can tell yourself that can provide emotional support and encourage you to face things in a positive way.

Some girls like to recite these out loud to themselves or write affirmations where they would see them throughout the day. Here are five suggestions to practice saying to yourself. Try reciting them before school and maybe even during the school day. The more you practice, the more powerful they become.

1. I am a great person.
2. I don't have to face my challenges alone.
3. I am supported, valued, and loved.
4. I am worthy of joy and laughter.
5. I am happy just the way I am.
6. I communicate through honesty and love.
7. I create joy for others every day.
8. I have a brave heart.
9. I don't let things bother me.
10. I am thinking clearly.

# Social World, Happy You

It's exciting to get connected and involved. When you have a passion for something and you meet other girls who share that same passion, great friendships can form. Whether on sports teams, during art activities, or in academic clubs, being connected can help distract you from mean behavior happening and help you focus on things that are the most important to you.

You've probably seen this before, but when a group of girls gets together, no matter which activity they're doing, mean behavior can start boiling up. Usually, at least one person ends up getting their feelings hurt and being left out. What can we do to shift this? It all starts with being the change! Take it upon yourself to say something when it's needed, always include others, and speak kind words to build others up. Use your club or organization as an opportunity to build your leadership skills.

What happens if it's your friend who's doing the bullying behavior? This seems tricky when you first think about it, but it's really not. The classic bully repeatedly hurts you because they want to gain power and control over you. They do this to get at you physically, emotionally, or verbally. If this is happening from a friend, they might not be as good of a friend to you as you thought. When hanging out with friends turns into a "them against you" scenario, it's probably not the best place to be hanging out.

If you are in a situation where you are hanging out with a group of friends and things are getting heated, what can you do to protect your image and not fall into the trap of being bullied? For starters, you can practice your assertive communication. Let them know in a respectful but stern way that they have crossed the line. This shows them that you still respect them as a friend but you will not put up with them treating you badly. Another option is to partner up with another girl in your group who understands how you're feeling. This way you are still able to remain with your friend group but maybe not as close to the one being mean. If all else fails, you have every right to call an adult and go home. You still have the final say and deserve to feel valued and appreciated.

# CHAPTER 5

# NAVIGATING FRIENDSHIPS

**B**ullying can come from unexpected places and, as you learned in the last chapter, sometimes even our friends. In this section, you will uncover how changing social dynamics can play a role in bullying and find out what can help in different situations. This can look like coping with being left out, learning how to disagree respectfully, and moving on from a toxic friendship. Knowing how to cultivate healthy relationships can save you a lot of time navigating between good friends and those you might want to keep as acquaintances.

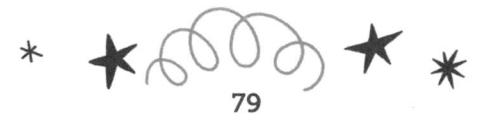

# Group Dynamics

Social circles can look remarkably similar or quite different, depending on several factors in life. One thing most of them have in common is that they can be used for the power of influence. This is interesting when it comes to bullying situations because our social circle can be extremely helpful or hurtful depending on who has power and control within it. Imagine a dartboard where you are at the center and there are rings all around you. These are your social circles. The ring closest to you is your family, the next one out is your friends, then your acquaintances, and the last one is other people in the community. The closer a person gets to you in the center, the more impact they have in your life and the greater power of influence you can have on each other.

Navigating social circles can be one of the toughest parts of adolescence. There are different kinds of groups all around you. If the group seems like a good fit, there are times when inserting yourself in the conversation or activity seems like a great idea. Using your social circles, you may begin joining the same groups as your closest friends or inviting them to join groups you're interested in. Understanding that everyone has a different set of social circles is important because who's influencing your friend might not be influencing you.

Jolene and her sister are close. Her sister is a couple years older, but they do everything together. She fits very closely in Jolene's social circle—in fact, she is one of the closest people to her. After school one day, her sister decided to ride home with some friends and asked Jolene to come, too. They both knew they weren't supposed to do that, but their parents wouldn't be home for another two hours. Against her better judgment, Jolene got in the car with her sister and her friends.

This is an example of someone close in your social circle who can have a greater influence in your life. Scan your social circles. Draw them out and write who is in each ring; then look at patterns of people who hold influence in your life. Close people like our family can be one of the best support networks we have, but there are times—like Jolene experienced—when you might have to pull your power and influence to do what's right.

## Odd Person Out

No one likes being left out. Whether it's a big group or a small circle of friends, there's nothing worse than not being included. Earlier in this book, we talked about your ability to have control over your own choices. Sometimes you need to look at what you can control and not focus on things you can't. For example, we can't control other people and what they choose to do. In this section, we will look at some things you can do to take back your control when you feel left out.

For starters, make sure you're practicing your social skills. In a small group, plug yourself in by joining the conversations. This can help you feel more included and let others know you're interested in joining. Sometimes being left out can be your perception of the situation, but it might not be what's actually happening. There are times when conversations go still and girls might not have much to say. During these moments, it can be easy to assume you're being left out, but that's not always the case. Survey the crowd to see if there's a way you can get plugged in. You might be surprised how the tables can turn.

If you've assessed the situation and you still feel they are definitely leaving you out on purpose, there are some other things you can do to regain your control, like giving them space. If you are with friends and you're needing to break free from the group, ask someone you relate to more to come with you. You can explain how you're feeling, and they can support you in the conversations and activities.

No one deserves to be treated this way. Get plugged into groups that include you and make your heart happy. You want to feel like a valuable part of the group, so make your choices count.

# Write Away the Rotten

Many girls face feelings of isolation when they are excluded from a group or from a few close friends. Think about a time when you were left out or picked on. On a separate piece of paper, write down those feelings. With this exercise, you are dumping all the negativity from this experience onto your piece of paper. Okay, now that you've written it down, go to the trash can. You're about to tear those feelings up and let them go! With each tear, say one positive thing about yourself until the entire paper is ripped up in the trash can. Come back to this page and write down how the activity made you feel. List some ways you could respond next time something like this happens to you.

- - - - - - - - - - - - - - - - - - - - - - - - - - - - - - - - - - - - - - - - - - -

- - - - - - - - - - - - - - - - - - - - - - - - - - - - - - - - - - - - - - - - - - -

- - - - - - - - - - - - - - - - - - - - - - - - - - - - - - - - - - - - - - - - - - -

- - - - - - - - - - - - - - - - - - - - - - - - - - - - - - - - - - - - - - - - - - -

- - - - - - - - - - - - - - - - - - - - - - - - - - - - - - - - - - - - - - - - - - -

- - - - - - - - - - - - - - - - - - - - - - - - - - - - - - - - - - - - - - - - - - -

- - - - - - - - - - - - - - - - - - - - - - - - - - - - - - - - - - - - - - - - - - -

# Crushes and Bullying

Do you know a friend who likes to repeat personal things you've told them? You know, the person who reveals your secrets just because they want others to laugh or to make you look silly or because they want to control the situation? Some girls have horrible experiences with others who reveal their school crushes. Chances are, if you haven't had experience with this yet, over the next few years you will encounter some form of this bullying.

As girls grow older, crushes can happen, and everyone is entitled to like who they like. If you have a crush, it's best to keep it to yourself unless you're okay with the news getting out. Even if you completely trust your friend, sometimes these new social dynamics can influence what someone does with that information. So if you absolutely do not want anyone to know, don't say it out loud. If you feel the need to share, seek out a trusted adult.

You may be wondering what you can do if people find out about your crush. Take time to think about what's going on and why. Is someone making fun of a crush you have because the other person doesn't feel the same way? Or is someone being mean because they have the same crush? Think about these scenarios carefully because what you can do depends on what's happening. Try talking to your friend about it or being up front with the person you have a crush on. If the mean behavior and drama continue, try shifting your focus to other things and not spending time worrying about your crush. You have plenty of time to get crushes figured out—you don't need to spend your time worrying about that now. Start building a crush on yourself!

# Growing Pains

As girls grow older, they start to see a shift in other people, including themselves. These growing pains are a normal part of life and, in a sense, are a way of finding who you are as a person. You develop throughout the years with a set of morals, values, and beliefs about what your life should look like and how you should live it. Sometimes as you're meeting new people and learning more, you are sorting through what fits and what doesn't fit within your system of life. If someone is acting outside the values you have set for yourself, you might decide you don't want any part of that. This is normal—in fact, you're doing this every day without even knowing it.

It's important to have a solid foundation in order to handle friendship changes. If you are having trouble sailing through this aspect of life and you're not sure what set of guidelines you're arranging for yourself, make sure to talk to your family, one of your trusted adults, or a school counselor. They can help you clear up some confusion and get you back on track for strong, healthy friendships.

Having a shift in friends can make things seem lonely at times. Use the strategies in earlier sections and find the courage to put yourself out there. School can be a challenging environment, even when you're using the tips and trying your best. There are also other opportunities to meet new people. Try becoming active within a different organization in your community. Sometimes there are girls there who don't attend your school but share the same values and interests as you.

## Changing Hobbies and Interests

Life takes girls in all different directions. Don't be afraid if one day you enjoyed an activity and a couple years later you don't like it. Your amazing personality develops over time and molds what you are interested in. No matter what personality changes you're experiencing, there is always something you can get involved in.

Growing up, Lizzy watched her aunt be an all-star volleyball player and wanted to be just like her. She knew when the time came, she would eat, sleep, and breathe volleyball. Lizzy got that opportunity in third grade when the elementary sports packet was released. She spent the next four years investing tons of time in volleyball practices, camps, and traveling teams. Things went well for a while and Lizzy enjoyed playing, but there was a noticeable transformation in relationships, communication, and support once she started getting older. Lizzy quickly learned she didn't like heated confrontation. She made the hard decision to quit volleyball once she reached junior high.

To this day, Lizzy still loves the game of volleyball and understands that she didn't like the social dynamics of this specific group of players. It promoted an unhealthy view of others, caused some mean behaviors, and had several instances of exclusion. Lizzy realized it wasn't the sport that caused these feelings—it was the social dynamics of the people. She enjoyed being part of a team, so she decided to look for a more inclusive set of girls who focused on building others up. She joined the cheer team and has made some incredibly supportive friends who build one another up to be their personal best. All it took was understanding what she liked and what she did not and then scanning her possibilities to find a great fit.

# Have You Ever Lost a Friend?

Does it seem like your friend has moved on? If your friend isn't returning the effort and seems like they aren't interested, it might be time to let the friend go. Ask yourself these questions to see if it's time to move on from a friendship. Write down your thoughts.

1. Are you always the one to start a conversation?

2. Does it seem like you have less in common now?

3. Does your friend want to socialize with other people?

----------------------------------------

----------------------------------------

----------------------------------------

----------------------------------------

----------------------------------------

----------------------------------------

----------------------------------------

----------------------------------------

# Five Tips for When They Move On

**Find the good.** There's a lot that goes into ending a friendship, and it's easy to become overwhelmed with the things that went wrong. Try to think about the good qualities. Are there things you want to look for in your next friend or even try to do better yourself?

**Process how you feel.** Don't be afraid of your feelings. This is hard, so take the time to process and heal. Write in a journal, be creative, or talk to someone who understands where you're coming from.

**Connect to your support system.** There are people surrounding you who love and support you. Look within your family structure, your school environment, and social organizations to find support. They will be your own support system for you to move forward.

**Know your limits.** Friendships are a two-way street. One person can't do all the heavy lifting. Communication is key when it comes to navigating friendships further. Be open and honest with yourself the next time around.

**Look for other friend groups.** Get involved to make positive change. Partner with someone new during lunch and try inviting an acquaintance to do something over the weekend. These things could lead to a more developed friendship.

# The Frenemy

Do you know someone who is nice to your face but mean behind your back? They may come across as your friend when you are in a class together without any onlookers. But the minute you step into the hallway around everyone else, they act like you don't exist. That's a frenemy!

Some more ways to spot a frenemy would be if they only want to talk about themselves, they often ask you to do favors for them, and their jokes are hurtful. Overall, a friendship with a frenemy just makes you feel bad.

The good news is that you get to decide how to handle it. You must love and respect yourself, so don't feel bad about putting yourself first. It's okay to tell the other person no, create boundaries, and be honest with them.

# Disagreement Is Part of Life

There's never going to be a time when every person on earth agrees 100 percent about something. In fact, disagreeing is a normal part of relationships. You want to be able to talk about things without the other person getting upset. Also, you want your feelings to be heard and valued, even if the other person doesn't agree. Learning to disagree now will set you up for lifelong success at resolving conflicts.

In life, you will experience times when there are respectful conflicts and others where feelings get hurt. Most of the time when someone takes time to hear your ideas and disagrees with them, they are not against you or out to destroy your opinion. They just simply don't have the same view and that's okay. The world would be a boring place if everyone had the same opinion about things.

With healthy conflicts come good communication, problem-solving, and active listening. Both parties should make sure to remain calm and try to view the situation from the other person's shoes, using phrases like "I understand how you would think that" and "It must feel horrible if you thought that's what happened." Finding common ground can help resolve the issue. Take time to understand how they feel; then express your feelings and ask, "What can I do to make things better?"

When a conflict is one-sided, unhealthy and toxic behavior can develop. It's when the other person won't take the time to listen to your viewpoint and they are not willing to take the steps to fix the problem. What they want is for you to always give in, follow their lead, and not disagree with them. This kind of relationship is hurtful and wrong. Always take time to hear others out, value their opinions, and learn to disagree respectfully.

# CHECKING IN

It's time to check in with yourself and how you feel about what you've learned. What are the five biggest takeaways from these chapters that you could share with a classmate or friend?

1. _____

_____

_____

2. _____

_____

_____

3. _____

_____

_____

4. _____

_____

_____

5. _____

_____

_____

# SEEING HER

Adalia and Mal were best friends and ate lunch together every day. At least that's what Adalia thought until one day at lunch when an upsetting situation happened. Mal decided she wanted to sit with another group of girls. They ignored Adalia and said mean things. So Adalia wrote Mal a note to explain she understood wanting different friends but that the ignoring and bad comments made her feel hurt. From that point, she started hanging out with another friend who was in her dance class. Adalia realized that finding someone who shares her same interests and makes her feel good is way more important than just trying to fit into a group.

If you were Adalia writing the note to Mal, what would you have said to express how you were feeling?

------------------------------------------------

------------------------------------------------

------------------------------------------------

------------------------------------------------

------------------------------------------------

# Healthy vs. Unhealthy Fights

| HEALTHY CONFLICTS | UNHEALTHY CONFLICTS |
|---|---|
| Problem-solving with the bully to find a good solution | Getting defensive when the bully tries to state her opinion and express herself |
| Listening to her side to better see her point of view | Using words that criticize and judge the bully for her behavior |
| Expressing how I feel to this person in a way that doesn't blame her | Gossiping with others first, before talking to the bully |
| Staying calm and respectful while communicating with the bully | Believing my side of the story is always the right side |
| Finding common ground and compromise | Posting things about the bully on social media before talking to her in person |

Let's test what we've worked through in this chapter with a short true/false quiz.

1. Telling others about our disagreement will help the person I'm arguing with see my point.
   **True / False**

2. Listening to my friend and staying calm will help me express my opinions next.
   **True / False**

3. Telling the other person how I feel and working to understand their feelings will help us compromise and work together.
   **True / False**

4. Even when a conflict is one-sided, you can still have a healthy conversation with the other person.
   **True / False**

5. When you decide to end a friendship, it's important to connect to your support system.
   **True / False**

1. False 2. True 3. True 4. False 5. True

# CHAPTER 6

# STANDING UP FOR OTHERS

**N**ow that you are becoming more comfortable standing up for yourself, try to extend this new confidence to other people. Standing up for others is an extremely important part of putting an end to bullying situations. You can rise above bullying to support your friends, classmates, and people you don't even know. If you see something that's not right, use your newfound confidence to change it and speak up. Other girls need you to stand strong and set confident examples—just think about how different bullying would look if all girls did this for one another. Be the supportive friend that you needed.

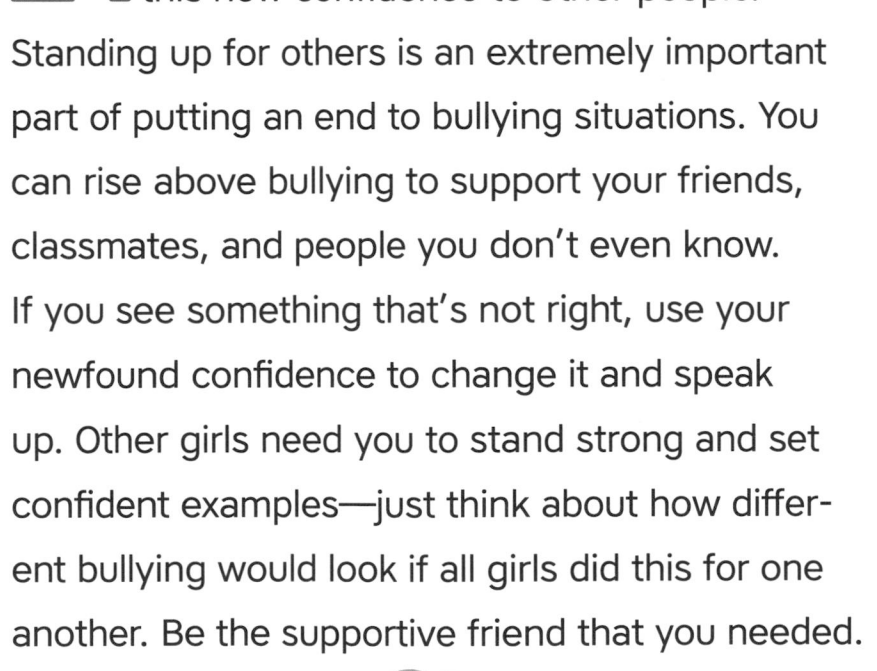

# Becoming an Anti-Bullying Pro

Anti-bullying means you are completely against bullying toward you or anyone else. It is being willing to take a stand against the wrongdoings of others and being brave enough to voice it somehow. You have learned so much throughout this book, so now is the time to create your plan and become an anti-bullying pro!

Think about how wonderful it would be to sit down at the lunch table where people acknowledge each other and greet each other with a smile. Or to walk through a hallway full of laughter and positive affirmations. Do you think a world could exist where the unity of sisterhood never breaks and brave girls always stand with one another? Are you getting goose bumps yet? This is sounding so amazing!

A shift in perspective takes action to get it accomplished. You can do all the wishing and imagining you want, but all it takes is one small act each day. Together, those actions will build your stamina to do more and more. It's like throwing a rock in a pond and watching the ripples spread—your one anti-bullying act can lead to more. It can empower others to do what is right. You can be bigger than yourself by giving others the courage it takes to defend their rights. Remember, everyone has the right to be themselves and feel valued.

Are you ready to do something big to make a greater impact? Team up with other classmates and talk to your school counselor, principal, or school board. Work with someone to join or organize an anti-bullying group at your school. This can promote a powerful movement where others will want to invest their time into helping. Get the word out by creating informational posters, speaking at assemblies, gathering research, and, most important, living it by example.

The nonprofit organization Kind Campaign created a movement to end "girl-against-girl" bullying and to encourage love, acceptance, inclusivity, and kindness. They created shirts that say "You Can Sit with Us." Imagine what it would be like to go into a cafeteria where all the girls are wearing these. The stress, anxiety, and heartache of not knowing who would allow you to sit with them would be a thing of the past. This is the future we need, for every single girl.

To read more about this amazing campaign and bring Kind Clubs to your community, check out KindCampaign.com.

## Standing Up for Friends

You will encounter times when you really want to help a friend in need. You hold the power to make change for the better. In these situations, it is best to remain calm and act quickly. Your brain is wired to do one of three things: flee, fight, or freeze. You don't want to be a bystander and freeze. You also don't want to get overheated and physically fight. Instead, practice for when this happens and let your brain know what to do in situations like this.

If you see your friend encountering a bullying situation, remain calm, assert yourself, and remove your friend by taking them away. They may be the one frozen or ready to fight. Since you are not the target, it makes you a perfect support system to think more clearly. Once you get them away from what's happening, talk to them about it. Take time to hear their feelings and see how you can help. If this is something that has been happening for a while and has the potential to become dangerous, get help from a trusted adult. This way, your friend will have more support and the ability to talk out her feelings with someone who can intervene more if needed.

There's another amazing way to take action. If anti-bullying efforts are rippling through your school and organizations, make a bully bubble! Create this bubble so big that bullies can't bust through. Gather everyone together and buddy up, sit together at lunch, travel the halls together, and spend time together during free time. This bubble of friends will be the biggest way to bust a bully in their tracks.

Want to take it a step further? They might be deeply seeking an inclusive group like yours. Just make sure to lead with love while maintaining safe friendship boundaries.

Friends need one another and girls all over the world need the connection of sisterhood to have the courage to stand up against bullying behavior. Practice what to do if you see a friend in need and be ready to act.

# What's the Best Way to Support?

1. I put myself in the girl's shoes to try to understand what that would feel like. **Helpful / Hurtful**

2. I ask her how I can help. **Helpful / Hurtful**

3. I tell someone in class that she has a crush on them. **Helpful / Hurtful**

4. When I talk to my classmate, I explain how I handled my situation and tell her what to do. **Helpful / Hurtful**

5. Throughout the day, I check on her to see how she is doing. **Helpful / Hurtful**

6. I understand I am not the person to solve everyone's problems. **Helpful / Hurtful**

7. Talking to others about a bullying situation helps give me ideas to help. **Helpful / Hurtful**

8. I show kindness to girls who have been bullied. **Helpful / Hurtful**

1. Helpful  2. Helpful  3. Hurtful  4. Hurtful
5. Helpful  6. Helpful  7. Helpful  8. Helpful

# Standing Up for Others

Taking a stand for others comes down to empathy. When you develop your empathy skills, you can start to imagine how it would feel if the behaviors were targeted at you. Even though it's not directed at you, you know the bullying behavior is wrong, and you want to do something to stop it. Some of the same tips and tricks will work when you decide to stand up for others in the same way you would for your friends.

Try to think of it like this: Wouldn't you want someone to stand up for you if you were in this situation? There are many ways you can do this and not be up in someone's face. Use your best judgment and decide if you need to be subtle or direct. If you decide to be subtle, try recruiting help from a teacher, coach, or close friend. This way the person can get the help they need without you broadcasting it to everyone. But if you need to act immediately and a direct approach is needed, try walking up to the person being bullied and saying something like "Hey, I've been looking all over for you." Then walk away with them, explaining that you were trying to help them out of that situation. They will probably think it's funny and will be glad you did.

Direct situations like this usually require more bravery, and you need to be willing to show your confidence. If you don't know the person being bullied, you may be worried about how they might respond. Will they allow you to stand up for them, or will they think you're being bothersome? Stop worrying about what others think. Bullying is wrong—you know it, and they know it. They will most likely appreciate the backup, and who knows, maybe you'll make a new friend in the process!

The same rules apply to classmates, teammates, and other students you may not know. It doesn't have to be perfect, just helpful—don't be afraid to act on it. These skills are important to develop and practice so that you can be a bully buster at any given point.

"Alone we can do so little;
together we can do so much."

*Helen Keller*

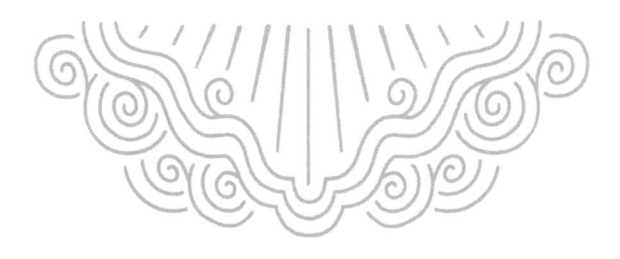

# SEEING HER

Marissa overheard a conversation in math about how the new girl Kera liked someone in their class. Marissa was embarrassed for Kera because she understood how it would feel to be humiliated. Even if it was true, Marissa knew Kera didn't want the class to know. During recess, Marissa asked Kera if there was anything she could do to help. Kera talked about how she doesn't know who's nice and whom to trust. She asked if she could sit by Marissa at lunch, and they instantly connected. Kera felt supported because Marissa was a friend she could talk to.

Do you have a friend like Marissa? If so, what makes them a supportive friend?

------------------------------------------------

------------------------------------------------

------------------------------------------------

------------------------------------------------

------------------------------------------------

# Stronger Together

Women and girls are better off when they respect and stand up for one another. It develops the unity we need as human beings so that we are bigger than we are alone. As much as some of us don't like to admit it, girls are social creatures who strive for connection and acceptance. Be the connection you're longing for—someone else might want it just as much as you do. Girls need to stop judging others and themselves, as it keeps them from unifying and forming strong bonds. Everyone needs acceptance and inclusion to accomplish this goal. In fact, girls need to see beauty in all different forms and connect without casting judgments.

This movement of acceptance can happen through empowerment, which is the process of becoming stronger and more confident. It's the power you give yourself or another person to do something big—that little spark that lights a flame inside you. Empowering yourself and others to make a change is where the shift happens, perspectives change, and girls start having eye-opening experiences within their social circles. They begin to recognize what works and what isn't working and then use their voice or actions to say so. It's not wrong to speak up as long as you lead with love and compassion for change.

Empowerment plays a role in standing up for one another because if you feel empowered and lead by example, you could light the spark that flames a fire in someone else. They see you doing it and think, *Hey, I can do that, too!* Empowerment spreads just like kindness to the point where it becomes contagious.

Right now, girls across the world need to make a pact to stand tall and brave, build others up, and unite to put an end to mean bullying behavior. Talk to the women in your life and have discussions on how they can help you. Discuss ways girls and women can band together and why it's important to talk these things out. Who knows, you may be the one to begin the next kindness movement.

# Power Inside and Out

Tune in to your own sense of power and let it radiate on the outside. It will help you connect with other girls! But you must be open to acknowledging differences and working out conflicts with other girls. Now, answer these questions.

1. How do you quiet your mind and listen to your inner self?

   ------------------------------------------------

   ------------------------------------------------

   ------------------------------------------------

   ------------------------------------------------

   ------------------------------------------------

2. What are some ways you can give yourself compliments and praise?

   ------------------------------------------------

   ------------------------------------------------

   ------------------------------------------------

   ------------------------------------------------

   ------------------------------------------------

→

**3.** How would you share your passions if your friend has a different view?

-----------------------------------------

-----------------------------------------

-----------------------------------------

-----------------------------------------

-----------------------------------------

**4.** What would it feel like to connect with other passionate, like-minded girls?

-----------------------------------------

-----------------------------------------

-----------------------------------------

-----------------------------------------

-----------------------------------------

**5.** What could you do right now to get connected?

-----------------------------------------

-----------------------------------------

-----------------------------------------

-----------------------------------------

# Friends and Sisters

Imagining your social circle, think about girls who fall close to you in the center and think about girls who are more toward the outside. There's no right or wrong position to be in when it comes to where people lie within your circles. It doesn't mean that you like someone more or less. This is just an image of where girls are in relation to how close they are to you in your life.

Now, with that in mind, imagine treating the girls who are further out of your circles with as much love, inclusion, and acceptance as you treat the girls closest to you in your circle. That would be an amazing feeling! Now imagine if other girls saw you as being that valuable to them, too. Don't you think that would empower a change, with all girls being valued at the same level? It would look like girls sticking up for one another all over the world!

We need to shift our perspective from thinking of others as either "in or out" and instead use a more accepting approach where everyone can be included equally. You can think of girls as your sisters in this world. All girls can be a part of a sisterhood where we build each other up and take time to learn about our differences. You want to know some great news? Girls are not all the same—and they shouldn't be! There are tons of variations in cultures, beliefs, personalities, interests, and more that make girls different. Taking time to learn, understand, and accept one another's differences will help foster inclusion.

This doesn't mean you need to accept everyone as your best friend and hang out with them every weekend. Naturally, our social circles are there for a reason based on our personal interests. But if someone needs to be included at lunch, recess, sport, or any other time, let them in and take time to make them feel valued. Everyone has a right to be seen and heard.

Start treating other girls as a part of the sisterhood. Get rid of the rating scale and start showing acceptance today, whether they are your actual sisters, close friends, acquaintances, or even the adult women in your life. All girls need to feel included and can join you in making a bigger impact for the better.

# "Believe in yourself, learn, and never stop wanting to build a better world."

*Mary McLeod Bethune*

# CELEBRITY SPOTLIGHT

Famous singer Rihanna told *Glamour* magazine that she was bullied for her skin color when she was a teenager. A few years later, she was bullied for her physical appearance. In the end she said she was grateful for what the experience taught her.

"Mean," one of Taylor Swift's hit songs, lets us in on a little piece of her past. According to an article by *People* magazine, she wasn't always the center of the spotlight. In fact, in junior high, a group of popular girls started leaving her out because she wasn't cool and pretty enough. That ended up being one of the motivators behind her ability to write songs. In later years, this group of girls was at a concert cheering her on, and Taylor decided to let things go and welcome in her newest fans. As she says, "Haters gonna hate." Just like Taylor uses her lyrics and music to speak, don't let others tear you down.

How are *you* going to speak up?

# Girl Power Is a Tool for Life

All girls have magical superpowers that help them navigate life and handle tough situations. When thinking about the word *superpower*, several other words might come to mind, like *courageous*, *honest*, *trustworthy*, and *kind*. These superpowers are what create superheroes, right? A superhero is someone who is an outstanding citizen within their community and brave enough to take a stand and make change for the better. These people are the good ones who fight for what's right.

Did you know your magic superpowers are what make you a hero? You don't have to take down villains or fight crime in the streets. What you choose to do with your superpowers can make a lifetime of difference for you and someone else. That single smile, one-time lunch buddy, or simple compliment at practice will have the power to change someone's life. You don't know what every girl is going through. Girls may be on a journey that is difficult to cope with and handle. Their bullying situation may be extremely hard to face, and the goodness you bring could empower them and give them hope.

Don't be afraid to be yourself. Find girls who are accepting. The more you plug in and get connected, the better off you'll be. Share this book with other girls who need a boost of courage to ward off bullies. Maybe even have a book club to tackle this topic at your school or organization. The more girls learn about this subject, the more inclusive and accepting the environment can be.

Gear up, grab your girlfriends, and unite the sisterhood because change is going to happen! Girls around the world, are you ready? This is your time! That spark is lit, so now you can fan the flames to ignite girl power. You deserve to be included. You have a right to use your voice for good. Use your tips, get connected with other girls, and do something to make positive change. You are amazing, and there is no doubt you're going to do great things!

# RESOURCES

*Cliques, Phonies & Other Baloney* **book:** Author Trevor Romain explains what cliques are, why they exist, and why they can be so annoying.

**Cyberbullying Research Center:** This website provides a variety of materials for both parents and teens to better explore the ins and outs of bullying. The site offers resources to overcome social media bullying, too. Visit cyberbullying.org/resources.

**The Kind Campaign:** This global nonprofit seeks to bring awareness and healing to the negative and lasting effects of girl-against-girl bullying. Visit KindCampaign.com.

**No Bully:** This organization promotes a kinder and more compassionate world to help end the crisis of bullying in schools and online. Visit NoBully.org.

*Wolfpack* **book:** Two-time Olympic gold medalist and FIFA World Cup champion Abby Wambach inspires the next generation to find their voice, unite their pack, and change the world.

# REFERENCES

"11 Facts about Bullying." DoSomething.org. Accessed May 28, 2021. DoSomething.org/us/facts/11-facts -about-bullying#fn2.

"Bullying Statistics." National Bullying Prevention Center. Accessed May 28, 2021. Pacer.org/bullying/info /stats.asp.

"Cyberbullying." National Bullying Prevention Center. Accessed May 28, 2021. Pacer.org/bullying/info /cyberbullying.

Davis, Stan, and Charisse Nixon, PhD. "The Youth Voice Project." The Pennsylvania State University. 2010. NJBullying.org/documents/YVPMarch2010.pdf.

Ditch the Label. "Why Do People Bully? The Scientific Reasons." Ditch the Label. November 15, 2020. us.DitchTheLabel.org/why-do-people-bully.

"Facts about Bullying." StopBullying.gov. Last modified August 12, 2020. StopBullying.gov/resources/facts.

Kadushin, Charles. "Power, Influence and Social Circles: A New Methodology for Studying Opinion Makers." *American Sociological Review* 33, no. 5 (October 1968): 685–99. JSTOR.org/stable/2092880.

"Learning from Student Voice: Bullying." YouthTruth. Accessed May 28, 2021. YouthTruthSurvey.org /bullying.

Lickteig, Beverly. "Social Media: Cyberbullying, Body Shaming, and Trauma." The Child Advocacy Center of Lapeer County. Accessed May 28, 2021. CACLapeer .org/social-media-cyberbullying-body -shaming-and-trauma.

Messer, Lesley. "Taylor Swift Suffered Bullying in School." *People*. December 1, 2020. People.com/celebrity /taylor-swift-suffered-bullying-in-school.

Patchin, Justin W., and Sameer Hinduja. "Tween Cyber-bullying in 2020." Cyberbullying Research Center and Cartoon Network. 2020. i.CartoonNetwork.com /stop-bullying/pdfs/CN_Stop_Bullying_Cyber_ Bullying_Report_9.30.20.pdf.

US Department of Education. "Student Reports of Bully-ing: Results from the 2017 School Crime Supplement to the National Crime Victimization Survey." July 2019. NCES.ed.gov/pubs2019/2019054.pdf.

"What Is the Definition of Verbal Bullying and What Are the Effects of Verbal Bullying?" BRIM Anti-Bullying Software. Accessed May 28, 2021. AntiBullying Software.com/what-is-the-definition-of -verbal-bullying.

# Acknowledgments

Thank you to everyone who believed in my abilities to write this book. It was a pleasure to work with such an amazing team to accomplish something so important. The thought of having this in the hands of young girls set my heart on fire for them. More than anything, I wanted to be an empowering voice that lets them know they can do big things. This opportunity was amazing, and I am blessed to have been a part of it.

# About the Author

**Jessica Woody** is a wife and a mom with two amazing kids. She is also a full-time professional school counselor, social-emotional curriculum writer, and a published author. With more than a decade of education experience, Jessica has developed a unique voice that empowers children and adults to be their best selves. She is the mastermind behind the blog *Simply Imperfect Counselor*, where she brings that same spark to like-minded professionals. Jessica has a master's degree in school counseling and was regionally awarded the Elementary School Counselor of the Year award in 2019. Find her online at SimplyImperfectCounselor.com.